VOL 25   APRIL 2023

BUSINESS
SLAY MONTHLY MAGAZINE

I0513179

10 KEYS TO SUCCESS

DARE TO DREAM.

START UP
and how to start it.

HOW TO
GROW YOUR BUSINESS

"Don't Wait for an Opportunity, Create it."

Exclusive Interview with the CEO Crystal Bedassie

WWW.SLAYMONTHLYMAGAZINE.COM

Issue 25 SLAY MONTHLY

BUSINESS MAGAZINE

Crystal Bedassie is an New York Native who is the CEO that founded Slay Monthly Magazine in 2020 now known as Project Slay Productions X Slay Monthly Magazine as of January 2023 based out in Oklahoma City. Slay Monthly Magazine is an digital/print monthly publication that focuses on businesses, beauty, fashion, and entertainment within the American community. The magazine has currently been rebranded since 2020. Crystal Bedassie has always been creative and had a passion for the arts. At the age of 15, she began to develop her skills as a makeup artist. After high school, she attended the University of Phoenix where she majored in Mass Communications, and Business Management. During her time in college, she realized that there was a lack of representation of urban American women in the media. She decided to take matters into her own hands and created Slay Monthly Magazine.

www.slaymonthlymagazine.com

BUSINESS NEWS

Our Mission For Project Slay Productions X Slay Monthly Magazine LLC was to be able to give creators from Models, Photographers, Brands & Businesses to have a platform to not only showcase their work, fashion, products and services, and talents but to help them grow in their careers & gain opportunities and recognition without having to pay thousands of dollars, by giving them a chance to gain massive exposure throughout social media to help them make money on platforms such as Facebook, Instagram, TikTok and many more to all depends on you, especially for creators who are seeking to get monetized on these platforms!! In a year alone we grew our brand where we published creators and businesses worldwide and our publication reached every state In The USA, including The UK, Japan, Germany, Canada, India, Italy, Mexico, Australia, France, Brazil, Spain & The Netherlands!!! We Are Now expanding and taking Slay Monthly Magazine to the next level. We are now on Amazon and Amazon Kindle and Roku and Vimeo showcasing interviews with models and owners of all kinds from every state. Our upcoming show footage will be featured on our Ruko channel, Vimeo, and Amazon Prime and live-streamed to our social media channels such as Instagram, Facebook, and YouTube, creating massive exposure to all models, brands & businesses to help them gain more potential supporters resulting In gaining more sales, & more followers guaranteed by collaborating with us. Project Slay Productions X Slay Monthly Magazine LLC is also a full-service advertising and media production company. We work with businesses, brands, and content creators to help them gain exposure in the media industry. We offer a wide range of services, including digital marketing, video production, and website design. Our team is dedicated to helping our clients achieve their goals and grow their businesses.

THE AWESOME GIFT GUIDE

We've added new items to our shop.
Visit our website to see our latest collections.

1. Headphones - $65 | 2. Slippers - $25 | 3. Candle - $12 | 4. Mug - $26 | 5. Scarf - $26
6. Crystals - $55 | 7. Books - $77 | 8. Plants - $25| 9. Jar - $55

WHY THE FUTURE IS OURS TO MOLD

AN INTERVIEW WITH MARK STANDERS BY CRYSTAL BEDASSIE

The future is ours to mold because the present is ours to shape. We can make the decisions today that will shape the future. We can choose to make the world a better place. We can choose to fight for justice. We can choose to stand up for what is right.

It is a blank slate that we can write on. We can choose what kind of future we want to create. . We can create the future we want to see. We have the power to make the future better than the past. We can choose to fight for a better future. You just have to want it bad enough.

It is often said that the future is ours to mold. But why is this the case? And what does it mean for the way we live our lives today? The future is ours to mold because, as human beings, we have the ability to shape and influence the world around us. We can do this through our actions, our words, and our thoughts. The future is also ours to mold because we have the power to make choices and decisions that will determine the course of our lives. We can choose to live in a way that contributes to the positive development of the world, or we can choose to live in a way that harms the planet and its inhabitants. The future is ours to mold because we are the custodians of the planet and its resources. We have a responsibility to care for the earth and its creatures, and to ensure that future generations inherit a world that is healthy and habitable. So, let's take this responsibility seriously and ensure that the future is indeed ours to mold!

the foodie week

happy me, happy food!

VOL. 2

DARE TO BE BOLD!

Show Off Your Style

FEATURING
OLIVIA WILSON ON THE ART OF

MIX & *Matching*

Are you looking for fashion tips that will help you look your best? If so, then you've come to the right place! In this article, we'll share with you our top fashion tips that will help you look stylish and feel confident.

SLAY MONTHLY MAGAZINE

First and foremost, it's important to understand your own personal style. What looks good on you? What colors do you feel most comfortable in? What styles flatter your figure? Once you have a good understanding of your own personal style, it will be much easier to put together outfits that make you look and feel your best

FASHION TIPS FOR EVERYONE

Next, it's important to invest in quality basics that you can mix and match to create a variety of different looks. A few versatile pieces that you can dress up or dress down will go a long way in your wardrobe.

Lastly, don't be afraid to experiment! Trying new things is the best way to find what works for you. So go ahead and experiment with different styles, colors, and silhouettes. And above all, have fun with fashion!

Fashion is an ever-evolving industry that is constantly changing to match the trends of the times. As such, it can be difficult to keep up with the latest styles and trends. However, there are some timeless fashion tips that everyone should know. Here are some essential fashion tips that will help you look your best no matter what the occasion.

Article written by Crystal Bedassie.

JUNE EDITION

HOW THE TRENDS ARE LEADING THE CHARGE

Interview by Neil Tran
Photography by Howard Ong

Trends are something that drives this world to move forward and make new breakthroughs. This is a fact that is happening in today's world. To take advantage of these moments, renowned fashion designer Isabel Mercado always puts forward creative ideas from the latest trends.

While trends can come and go, fashion that emerges from these trends can always have a chance to make a comeback, says Mercado. Therefore, she is never afraid even though the fashion she designs can seem seasonal.

DREW FEIG

REGISTER TODAY TO PERFORM AT NYFW

LETS GO!!!

We are seeking local talent for our upcoming NYFW Fashion Tour on September 9th 2023. To register go to www.slaymonthlymagazine.com

WWW.SLAYMONTHLYMAGAZINE.COM

How to be a Successful Digital Nomad

BY HARPER RUSSO

The life of a digital nomad is one that is often filled with Adventure and excitement. It can be a very rewarding experience, both professionally and personally. However, it is not a lifestyle that is without its challenges. In order to be successful as a digital nomad, there are certain things you need to keep in mind. Here are a few tips on how to be a successful digital nomad: 1. Create a Plan and Set Some Goals 2. Stay disciplined and Focused 3. Get organized and make use of Technology 4. Keep an open mind and be flexible 5. Have a positive attitude and believe in yourself If you can keep these things in mind, you will be well on your way to having a successful and rewarding experience as a digital nomad!

FRESH LOOK

OLIVIA WILSON

PROJECT SLAY PRODUCTIONS X
SLAY MONTHLY MAGAZINE

NYFW SLAY THE RUNWAY FASHOIN SHOW

SAVE THE DATE

9th Sept
1:30pm - 4:30pm

2023

Slay The Runway is a fashion Runway Show Tour that is recognized for providing a platform and a substantial audience that opens various opportunities & exposure to brands, businesses, designers, models, and performers of all kinds, and this year we are committed to making this event not just the years' most successful show, but our greatest show ever. To accomplish the task, we need help from supporters like you.

TICKET

Normal $25
VIP $99
Sponsorship Opportunities Available

Great for inspiring new models

CONTACT US

www.slaymonthylmagazine.com
slaymonthlymagazine@gmail.com

Vol. 25

WORKOUT
WORKOUT
WORKOUT
WORKOUT

CHOOSE MINERAL WATER FOR THE BODY WHEN EXERCISE

COCOA
• A SWEET EATS •

THE CHOCOLATIER

CHEF TONY'S NEW
SPECIALTY RESTAURANT
IS NOW OPEN

White Chocolate with Almonds

13 Dark Chocolate with peanuts

21 Truffles

Truffles are ectomycorrhizal fungi and are therefore usually found in close association with tree roots.

29 Coffee Craze

Coffee is a brewed drink prepared from roasted coffee beans, the seeds of berries from the Coffea plant.

PERFECTING THE IDEAL

Truffles

By **Miranda Stewart**
Photo by **Steve Greene**

Truffles are a type of fungi that grow underground, usually near the roots of trees. They are a highly sought-after ingredient in many cuisines, prestigious for their taste and exclusivity. Truffles are very difficult - and expensive - to cultivate, which is why they are often considered a luxurious ingredient. The most important part of cultivating truffles is training the truffle dogs. These dogs have an acute sense of smell, which is necessary to find the truffles hidden underground. Once the truffles are found, they must be carefully dug up so as not to damage them. Truffles are a rare and delicate ingredient, but if you're lucky enough to get your hands on some, they can make a dish truly special. Read on to learn more about how truffles are made, from start to finish.

all you need is love. but a little chocolate here and then doesn't hurt.

CHARLES M. SCHULZ

TRENDING

Coffee Craze

By Karl Plenton
Photo by Erica Yang

Coffee is one of the most popular drinks in the world. Millions of people drink coffee every day, and many of them can't imagine starting their day without a cup of coffee. But what is it about coffee that makes it so popular? Coffee has many benefits. It can improve your mood, and even help you burn fat. Coffee is also rich in antioxidants and can help you reduce your risk of some diseases. Studies have shown that coffee can help improve mental alertness and focus, as well as physical performance. Coffee is also a great source of antioxidants, which can help protect your body from damage from free radicals.

OWN YOUR STYLE!

SALFORD & CO.

DARE TO DREAM

WHY MAN ALWAYS LOVE BLACK

EDITOR *PICKS*

SLAYMONTHLYMAGAZINE.COM

HEALTHY SKIN	SKINCARE ROUTINE	MAKE UP TIPS
Healthy skin is smooth, with no breaks in the surface.	A Good things come to those who wait and that includes skincare routines	Before applying makeup, spread on a veil of a hydrating yet weightless moisturizer on clean skin

BEAUTY MAKE UP EDITION

BORCELLE

SUPERMODEL
IS BACK

FASHION IN 2023

Awareness of environmental sustainability does not only occur in the industrial and economic fields, but also in the fashion sector. Read how this awareness permeated the modern fashion industry and how it came about.

The concept of environmental sustainability is generally found in the culinary and lifestyle fields. Apparently, this concept has also begun to be taken seriously in the fashion industry. Also known as eco-fashion, various well-known fashion brands are starting to try to produce eco-friendly and renewable fashion products.

Having several characteristics such as being able to be recycled, being upcycled, cruelty-free, not made of chemicals that can pollute the environment, and others are some of the main advantages of this fashion compared to conventional fashion.

Written by Murad Naser

By Chad Gibbons

FAST FOOD

BURGER

www.slaymonthlymagazine.com

www.slaymonthlymagazine.com

Edition
25
April

Fashion
Top
Picks

SLAY
MONTHLY
MAGAZINE
Business And Lifestyle

BUSINESS

STEP UP YOUR BUSINESS

If you're looking to take your business to the next level, contact us. We can help you create a custom plan to improve your productivity, efficiency, and bottom line

HOW MAKE A STARTUP

First, you need to have a great idea for a product or service that people will want to buy. Second, you need to put together a team of talented and passionate people to help you turn your idea into a reality. Finally, you need to raise money to fund your business. If you're interested in

MEET THE LEADER CHAD GIBBONS

WORK HARD
PLAY SMART

www.slaymonthlymagazine.com

Bomber.

BOMBER JACKETS SOMETHING FOR EVERYONE

Previously only associated with men's clothing, now bomber jackets can be used by anyone, including women as well. Read about bomber jackets as a trend.

Written by Morgan Maxwell

In the past, bomber jackets were only used by fighter pilots who were all male. But then, this jacket began to be worn by civilians and its fame exploded when the nuances of valor and coolness of this jacket can now also be worn by ordinary people.

However, with the increasing number of female fighter pilots and the emergence of unisex fashion, this jacket can now be used by anyone. What was originally a men's outfit can now be worn by women too.

@slaymonthlymagazine

DESSERTS FOR YOUR SOUL

Guilt-free Brownies | Five Fresh Picks | Sweater Weather

THE STORY OF SACHA DUBOIS

Nightmare
Back To 1935

A place where the tragedy of the past begins,
making life take a critical turn.

LARANA INC.

Fauget Shoes
THIS SHOES IS YOUR STYLE

THE MOST WANTED SNEAKER

KEEPING UP WITH THE FUTURE

2023

VOL 25   APRIL 2023

BUSINESS
SLAY MONTHLY MAGAZINE

10 KEYS TO SUCCESS

DARE TO DREAM.

START UP
and how to start it.

HOW TO *GROW YOUR BUSINESS*

"Don't Wait for an Opportunity, Create it."

Exclusive Interview with the CEO Crystal Bedassie

WWW.SLAYMONTHLYMAGAZINE.COM

www.ingramcontent.com/pod-product-compliance
Lightning Source LLC
Chambersburg PA
CBHW041936240526
45473CB00034B/1725